Brilliant Support Activities

Understanding Materials

Alan Jones,
Roy Purnell,
Janet O'Neill

We hope you and your class enjoy using this book. Other books in the series include:

Understanding Light, Sound and Forces
printed ISBN: 978-1-78317-097-5
ebook ISBN: 978-1-78317-101-9

Understanding Living Things
printed ISBN: 978-1-78317-095-1
ebook ISBN: 978-1-78317-099-9

Published by Brilliant Publications
Unit 10
Sparrow Hall Farm
Edlesborough
Dunstable
Bedfordshire
LU6 2ES, UK

E-mail: info@brilliantpublications.co.uk
Website: www.brilliantpublications.co.uk
Tel: 01525 222292

Written by Alan Jones, Roy Purnell and Janet O'Neill
Designed and illustrated by Small World Design

The authors are grateful to the staff and pupils of Gellideg Junior School, Merthyr Tydfil for their help.

Printed ISBN 978-1-78317-096-8
Ebook ISBN 978-1-78317-100-2

First printed and published in the UK in 2014

10 9 8 7 6 5 4 3 2 1

Contents

Introduction to the series

This book shows the relevance and importance of understanding the science of everyday materials. The book is a series of activities to supplement any teaching you do on these topics and is designed for slower learners of any age but who are operating at the level of achievement normally associated with pupils at KS1 and KS2.

It is NOT a complete textbook on all aspects of the area of Everyday Materials.

The activities follow the guidelines of science concepts as outlined in the Programmes of Study of the National Curriculum (2014 edition) for years 1–3 and selected topics of year 4 and year 5. The activities should help to develop the essential Scientific Enquiry skills as outlined in the National Curriculum, namely those of 'Observation', 'Predicting', Recording', and 'Drawing Conclusions' through the activities included in the book.

The books contain a mixture of paper-based tasks and also some 'hands on' activities. The following symbols on each sheet have been used to indicate the type of activities.

What to do

Think and do

Read

Investigate

The sheets involving practical investigations use materials readily available in most schools or homes. The activities have been vetted for safety, but as with any classroom based activity, it is the responsibility of the classroom teacher to do a risk assessment with their pupils in mind.

The sheets generally introduce one concept area per sheet. They are designed to be used by single pupils or as a classroom activity if all the pupils are working in the same ability range. Alternatively they can be used as a separate sheet for slower learners working on the same topic as the rest of the class, hence helping differentiation within the topic area. They have also been found useful for pupils in hospital or who are away from school for prolonged periods. The sheets are easily modified for specific pupils or groups. They can be used in any suitable order as there is no hierarchy with the sequence in the books.

The sheets can be used for assessment purposes or homework tasks.

The sheets use simple language and clear black line illustrations to make them easy to read without colour distractions. They have reduced number of words and a straight forward vocabulary to help poor readers or pupils whose language skills might be limited. Written responses are required so helping writing and communication skills of pupils. The completion of the sheets can be done by a support teacher responding to a verbal or a sign instruction by the pupil. It is essential that all pupils feel a sense of success and achievement when doing science as it is part of their everyday life.

No particular reference has been made to any specific type of learning difficulty or disability as the material has been successfully tested with a wide range of pupils. The teachers can modify the method of use as the sheets can be enlarged or the instructions read onto a sound disc or computer. The sheets are easily converted to be shown on larger screens or computer screens.

The topics of this book match the New (and old) National Curriculum and cover the area of 'Everyday Materials' and help the pupils use the various processes and methods of science.

The worksheets in this book sometimes overlap with other activities but this will help the pupils to grasp the concepts in a different context. Some topics also take ideas from another science area just to show the links between the everyday science we use. The worksheets can be used in any suitable sequence as this is not a logical teaching scheme. They are designed to give flexibility and diversity to teachers with pupils working with a wide range of abilities within a class. Some topics have been chosen from the POS of year 4 to 6 but written with the slower pupils in mind. Other topics can be linked with geography, eg Rocks and minerals. Any numeracy work is at the lower levels of expectancy.

Some sheets encourage direct answers to specific questions whereas other activities require some degree of thinking before making a written response. The symbols on the sheets give an indication of this. The questions and presentation are simple but the level of pupil response can often reveal higher levels of understanding than expected.

National Curriculum POS and the Activities of this book

Because the New NC does not clearly indicate separate statements of the POS by using a nomenclature of numbering or letters within any areas it has been found convenient for OUR books to code and summarize these main sections of the NC. This will help the teacher see how the topics covered in this, and the other books in the series, cover the POS of the National Curriculum. They are all covered by the activities, some more than once.

New National Curriclum 2014

Letter headings are ours but refer to the NC statements quoted on the pages of NC

Processes needing to be covered:	Content of the POS
KS1 Our Summary of POS which are appropriate for Pupils both in Year 1 and Year 2, 'Working Scientifically', (WS) page 139 of NC. WSa Asking questions, and answering WSb Observing and using simple equipment WSc Testing ideas WSd Identifying and Classifying WSe Using observations to suggest answers WSf Gathering data to answer questions	**KS1 Our Summary of POS for Year 1 'Everyday Materials', (M) pages 141–142 of NC** M1 What are things made of? M2 Identifying everyday materials M3 Simple properties of everyday materials M4 Comparing different materials M5 Changing shapes of solid materials
The more elaborate 'Working with Science' POS generally used in Year 3 and Year 4 will be applied as necessary within the activities undertaken with the slower learners.	**KS1 Our Summary of POS for Year 2, 'Using Everday Materials' page146 of NC** M6 Identifying and comparing everyday materials M7 Comparing how things move on different surfaces
	Lower KS2 Our Summary of POS for year 3 and year 4 see page 149 of NC **year 3 Rocks see page 152 of NC** M8 Comparing rocks M9 How fossils are formed M10 What soils are made of M11 Solids, liquids, gases groupings M12 Changes of state with temperature M13 Water Cycle, evaporation and condensation

Links to the National Curriculum

Page Number	Title of Activity	National Curriculum Working Scientifically (WS)	National Curriculum Everyday Materials (M)
10	Natural or made?	a,d	M 1,2,4
11	Different materials	a,d	M 1,2,3,6
12	Made of what?	a,c	M 1,2 3 6
13	Water or not?	a,c,d,e	M 1,2,3
14	See-through properties	a,c,d,e	M 2,3,4
15	Gases	a,c,d	M 1,6,11,12,13
16	Liquids other than water	a,c,e.f	M 3,4,6
17	Solids	c,d,e	M 1,3,4,5
18	Float or sink?	a,c,d	M 1,3,4
19	Fizzy drinks	a,c,e,f	M 1,2,3,4
20	Ice and water	a,b,c,e,f,	M 3,4,5,6
21	Melting	a,c,e,f	M 1,3.4.6
22	Burning wood	a,b,e,f,	M 1,3,4,6
23	Barbeque heat	a,b,e	M 1,3 4 6
24	Stick to magnets	a,b,c,d,f	M 1,2,3,4,6 See also Physics areas P9,P10,P11
25	Rusting	a,b,c,d,e	M 1,2,3,4,6
26	Dissolving	a,b,c,d,e	M 1,2,3,4,6
27	Investigate dissolving	a,b,c,d,e,f,	M 2,3,4,5
28	Drinking chocolate	a,b,c	M 1,2,3,4,6
29	What happens to Smarties?	a,b,c,d,e,f,	M 1,3,5
30	Tea Bags	a,b,c,e,f,	M1,2,3,4,6
31	Filtering	a,b,c,e,f	M 1,2,3,4,6
32	Changes	a,c,e	M 1,2,3,6
33	Toasting bread	a,b,c,d,e	M 1,2,3,5,6
34	Changes to a flame	a,b,c,e,f,	M 1,2,3,5
35	What is changing	a,b,c,e	M 1,2,3,4,6
36	Burning candles	a,b,c,e	M 1,2,3,6
37	What is in the bubbles?	a,b,c,e	M 1,2,3,4,6
38	What is needed?	a,d,f	M 2,3,4
39	Compost	a,c,d	M 1,2,3,4,6
40	Water cycle	a,e	M 1,2,3,6,12,13
41	What happens?	a,b,c,e,f,	M 1,2,3,4,6
42	Snowman	a,c,e	M 1,2,3,4,5,6
43	Jelly and plaster	a,b.c.e	M 1,2,3,4,5,6
44	The lost ring	a,b,c,e,f	M 1,2,3,4,6
45	How much will dissolve?	a,b,c,e,f	M 1,2,3,4,6
46	Concrete	a,b,c,e,f	M 1,2,3,4,5,6
47	Hot and cold	a,b,c,e,f	M 1,2,3,4,5,6

48	Gases in liquids	a,b,c,d,e,f	M 1,2,3,4,6
49	Problem solving, 1	a,b,c,e,f	M 1,2,3,4,6
50	Problem solving, 2	a,b,c,e,f	M 1,3,4,6
51	Problem solving, 3	a,b,c,e,f	M 1,2,3,4,5,6
52	Problem solving, 4	a,b,c,e,f	M 1,2,3,4,6
53	Rocks, 1	a,b,c,d,e,f	M 8,9 10
54	Rocks, 2	a,b,c,d,e,f	M 8,9,10
55-56	Rocks, 3	a,b,c,d,e,f	M 8.9,10,12,13

Below are the possible answers to the problems and investigations for the activities on pages 49 to 52.

Page 49 Problem solving, 1 Sailor on the island

- The sailor can use the heat from the sun to evaporate the water from the salt water so slowly turning some into water vapour (salt does not evaporate). He could then hang a bottle of cold water over the hot salt water and as the water evaporated it will slowly condense on the cold outside surface of the bottle and form droplets of pure unsalty water. Let the pupils try this on a sunny day.

- The farmer should filter the water through muslin or a paper filter (like a coffee filter).

- The engineer could use a magnet as the steel girders can be detected through the plaster.

Page 50 Problem solving, 2 Simple thermometer

- Warming the water by holding the bottle in the hands, causes the water to expand and the water level in the tube to rise. Surrounding it with cold water or ice causes the level to fall. This is the principle of a thermometer.

- The wire when heated with a small candle flame (or sometimes with the heat from a radiator or hair dryer or in strong sunlight on a window sill) expands and the pointer goes up. The rule can be marked at different times of the day. The pivot can be counter balanced with a small weight (or plasticine) on the other side to get it to just balance or use a longer length of rod (to make it heavier) on the side opposite to the small weight.

Page 51 Problem solving, 3 Burning candle also Melting ice

- Candles use up oxygen when they burn, leaving behind unreactive nitrogen of the air (plus the products of the burning candle, mainly carbon dioxide); so the water level inside the jar will rise to take the place of the oxygen which has been used up.

- The water level will remain about the same as the ice cubes contract when they melt so taking up the space of the cube. Water expands when it freezes, that's why ice cubes float.

- The balance should remain about the same as the ice and the melted water have the same weight (mass).You can use a simple kitchen scales instead of the balance.

Page 52 Problem solving, 4 Rusting

- The air can be dried with a little bit of silica gel or simply warmed up. Rusting needs both moisture and oxygen (in the air) together. Make sure the nails are sandpapered or washed in detergent first as some are covered with a greasy layer to prevent rusting when bought.

- Air, particularly breathed out air in a cool bedroom, contains moisture which condenses on the cold windows.

- The iron gate has rusted in wet air (if not painted) and the limestone wall is attacked by acid rain (not so the clay brick). Old grave stones also wear away if they are made of marble or limestone.

Natural or made?

What to do

Draw a ring round **N** if the materials are natural.

Draw a ring round **P** if the materials are made by people.

N **P**

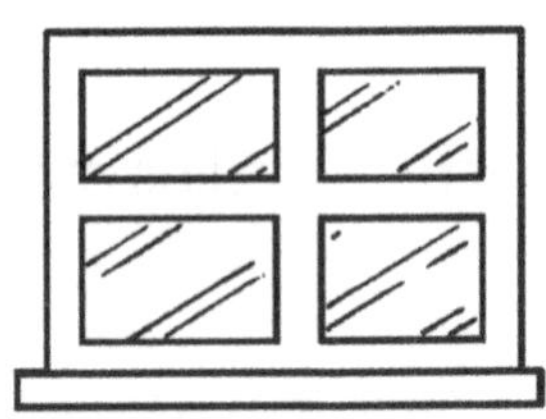

N **P**

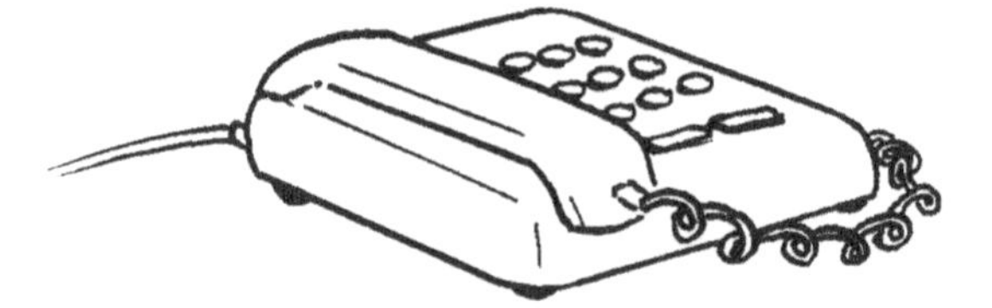

N **P**

N **P**

N **P**

Think and do

A cat is natural because ...

. . . .

. . . .

The cat food is **N** or **P** because . . . .

. . . .

Different materials

Read

There are thousands of materials in nature and even more made by people. You can colour the pictures.

What to do

Choose the correct words to write on each line:

natural **made by people**

A leaf on a tree is ....

A plastic bucket is ....

A mountain rock is ....

A screw is ....

An apple is ....

A paper clip is ....

Think and do

Choose the correct words to finish the sentence:

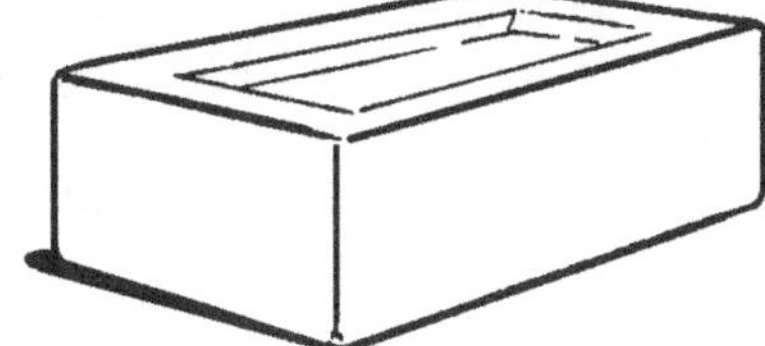

paper **plastic** **clay** **metal** **rough**

A house brick is made of baked .... Its outside feels ....

Made of what?

What to do

Draw a line from the picture to the material it is made of.

Metal

Brick

Paper

China

Glass

Think and do

Which thing came from the wood of a tree? ....

Are any of the things alive? ....

What is glass made from? ....

Water or not?

What to do

Choose the correct word to write on each line:

ice **water** **steam**

Rain is . . . .

A boiling kettle gives out . . . .

Snow is . . . .

An **iceberg** is . . . .

The cold drink has . . . . and . . . . in it.

Think and do

Water can be turned into ice by . . . .

Water can be turned into steam by . . . .

See-through properties

What to do

Do these things let light through? Draw a ring round **Yes** or **No**.

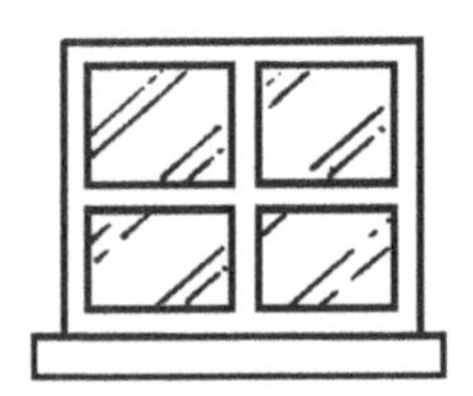

Glass of a window **Yes** **No**

Brick wall **Yes** **No**

Water **Yes** **No**

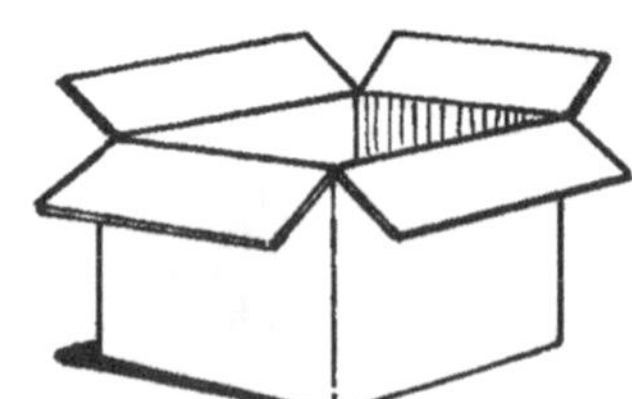

Cardboard **Yes** **No**

Balloon **Yes** **No**

Think and do

The window lets light through.

We say it is: **t** _ _ _ _ _ _ _ _ _ _

Cut out the letters and rearrange them to find the word.

r	a	n	s	t	t
r	a	n	e	p	

Gases

What to do

Write the correct word below each picture to show which gas is in the following things:

air **steam** **carbon dioxide**

Cola

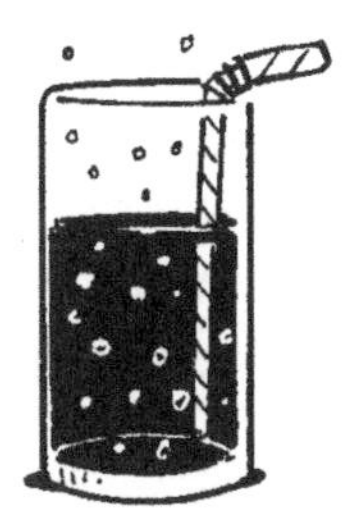

. . . .

Bubbles in a fish tank

. . . .

A boiling kettle

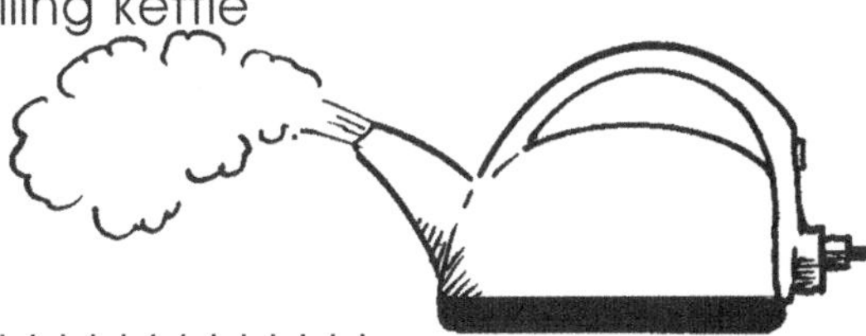

. . . .

A balloon

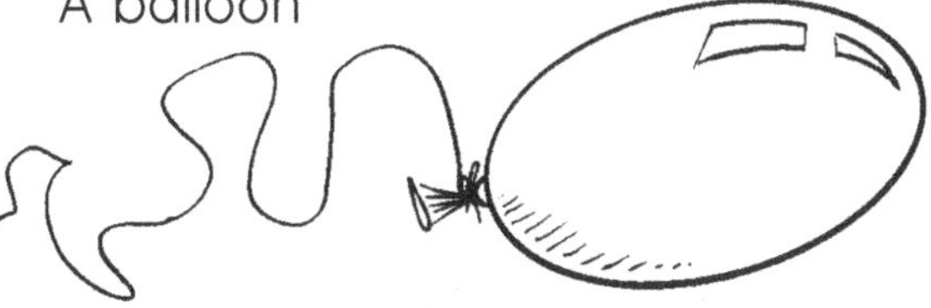

. . . .

An underwater diver

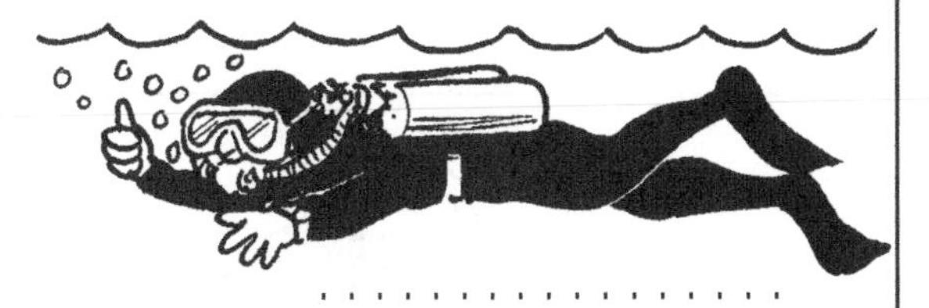

. . . .

A fire extinguisher

. . . .

Cooling towers at a power station

. . . .

Think and do

What gases do you breathe in? . . . .

What gases do you breathe out? . . . .

Liquids other than water

Read

Water, oil and washing-up liquid are all liquids.

Investigate

Try this:

Add 3 drops of
washing-up liquid.
Stir.

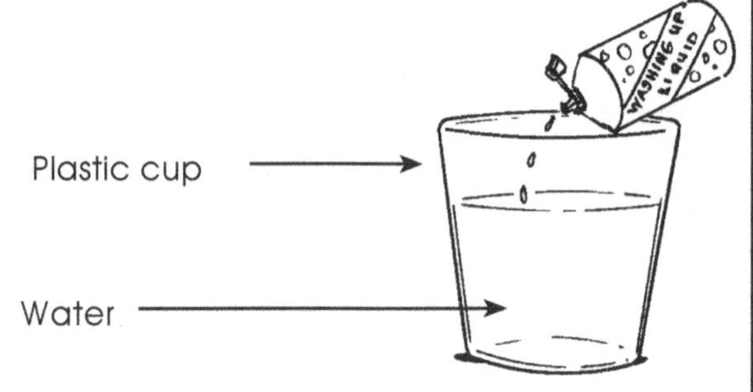

Do they mix? Yes/No

Add 3 drops of
cooking oil.
Stir.

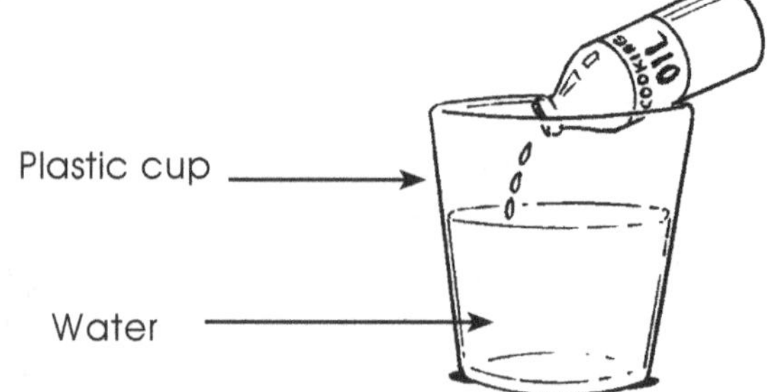

Do they mix?
Yes/No

Draw or write what happens now.
Add 3 drops of each and stir.

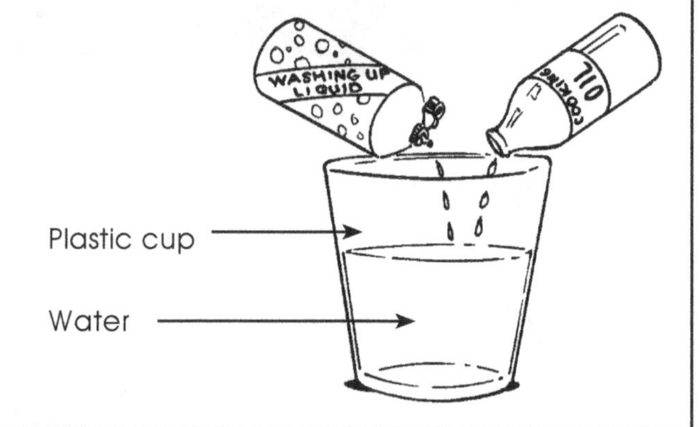

Think and do

Do these liquids have water in them? Write **Yes** or **No**.

Cooking oil . . . .

Cola . . . .

Cup of tea . . . .

Petrol . . . .

Solids

Read

A **solid** has its own shape. A piece of wood or an iron nail is a solid.
A **liquid** needs a container, such as a bottle, to hold it in.

What to do

Choose the correct word to finish each sentence:

solid **liquid**

Ice cubes are ....

Water is a ....

A block of soap is a ....

A loaf of bread is a ....

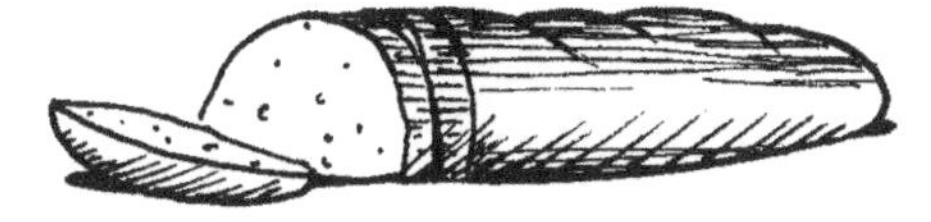

Cooking oil is a ....

Think and do

A piece of wood is sawn up.

Wood is a ....

because ....

Sawdust pieces are ....

Float or sink?

What to do

Write whether you think each thing will **float** or **sink** in water.

Ice will . . . .

A paper clip will . . . .

A coin will . . . .

A matchstick will . . . .

An iron nail will . . . .

An apple will. . . . .

A full can of cola will . . . .

An empty can of cola will. . . . .

You can investigate this if you wish, using a bowl of water.

Think and do

A heavy metal boat will float because

. . . .

. . . .

Fizzy drinks

Read

All fizzy drinks contain the gas carbon dioxide.

What to do

Look at a glass of clear lemonade. Answer these questions.

Where are the bubbles?

. . . .

Draw them.

Are all the bubbles the same size?

. . . .

What happens to the bubbles when they reach the top?

. . . .

. . . .

. . . .

. . . .

Think and do

What would happen to a currant or raisin if you added it to the lemonade?

If you do the experiment, remember to record all you see.

I saw . . . .

Arm bands help you to float in a swimming pool because . . . .

. . . .

. . . .

Ice and water

Investigate

Take a coloured ice cube or piece of iced lolly and add it to water.
Do not stir. Watch and draw what happens.
Colour the picture.

Think and do

Try again using warm water. Draw what happens.

Coloured ice cube

I think this happens because. . . . .

. . . .

. . . .

Melting

Read

It is a hot day and Sally's ice cream begins to melt in the sun.

What to do

What could Sally do to stop the ice cream from melting so fast?

. . . .

. . . .

Think and do

Why doesn't ice cream melt when inside the freezer in the shop?

. . . .

. . . .

. . . .

What material would be good to wrap a carton of ice cream in to carry it home?

. . . .

. . . .

. . . .

Name some things that should be kept in a fridge or freezer to stop them melting.

. . . .

. . . .

. . . .

Burning wood

Read

This is a barbecue, made of steel.

The fuel was wood and it got very hot.

The sausages grilled well.

What to do

Explain what changed during the barbecue.

The wood changed to . . . .

. . . .

The pink sausages changed to . . . .

Why does the steel not melt? . . . .

Think and do

Where did the different smells come from?

. . . .

. . . .

. . . .

Barbecue heat

Read

This is a barbecue, made of steel.

The fuel was wood and it got very hot.

The sausages grilled well.

What to do

Why did the cook use a long metal fork with a wooden handle?

. . . .

. . . .

Why does the cook wear gloves, glasses and an apron?

. . . .

. . . .

What happens if the sausages are left on the barbecue too long? . . . .

. . . .

Think and do

This sausage is inside a bun.

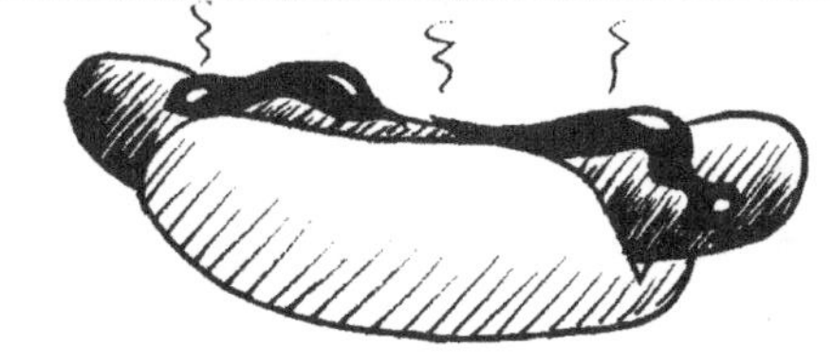

Will it burn your fingers? . . . .

. . . .

Two materials that are good heat insulators are . . . .

and . . . .

What other things could be barbecued? . . . .

. . . .

Stick to magnets

What to do

Put a tick ✓ in the box next to the things you think a magnet would 'stick' to.

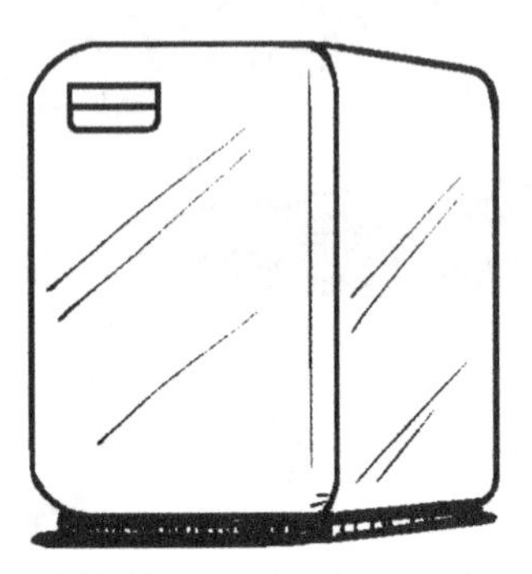

☐ Fridge door

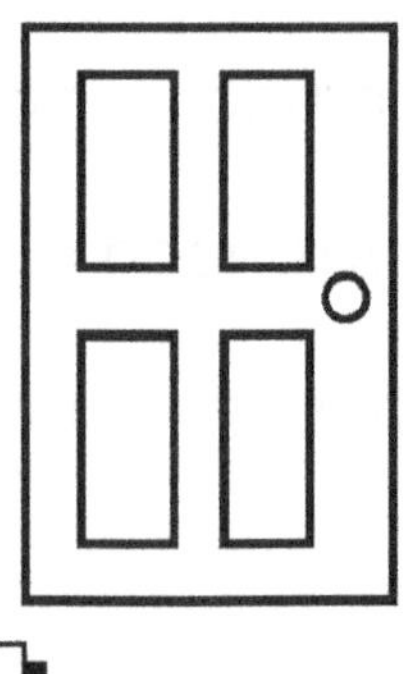

☐ Wooden door

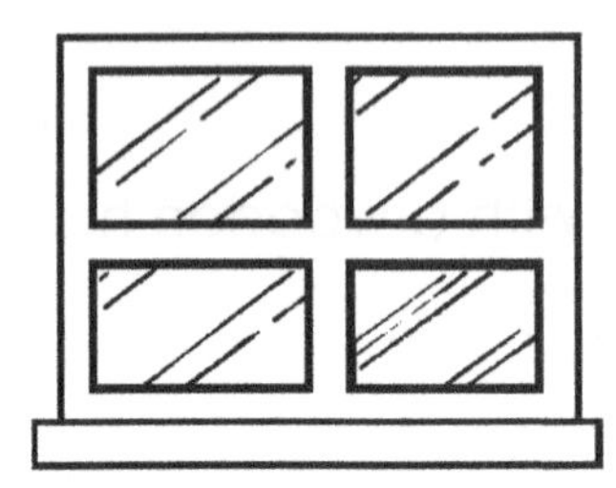

☐ Glass window

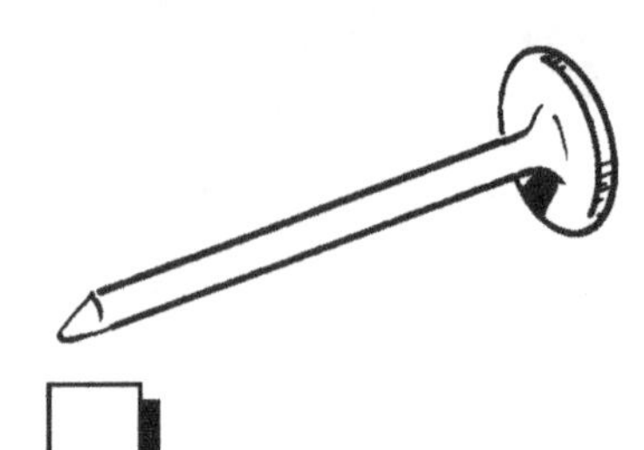

☐ Nail

☐ Newspaper

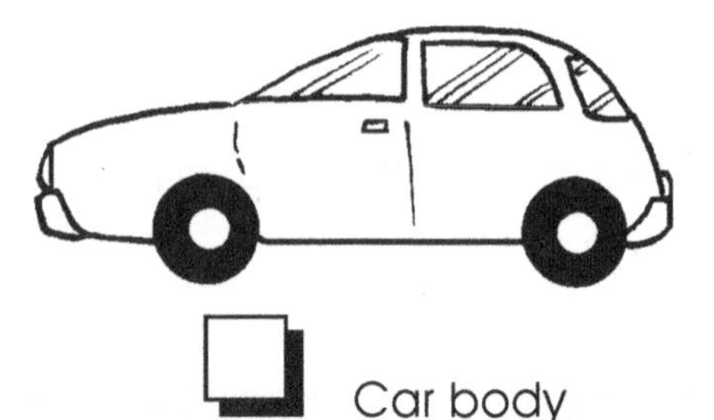

☐ Car body

☐ Plastic bag

You can investigate this using a magnet.

Think and do

Do you think a magnet will 'stick' to a drinks can?

Try it and see.
Are all metals magnetic? . . . .

Rusting

Read

Rusting happens when things made of iron are left out in the air and rain.

What to do

Put a tick ✓ in the box by the things that you think will rust.

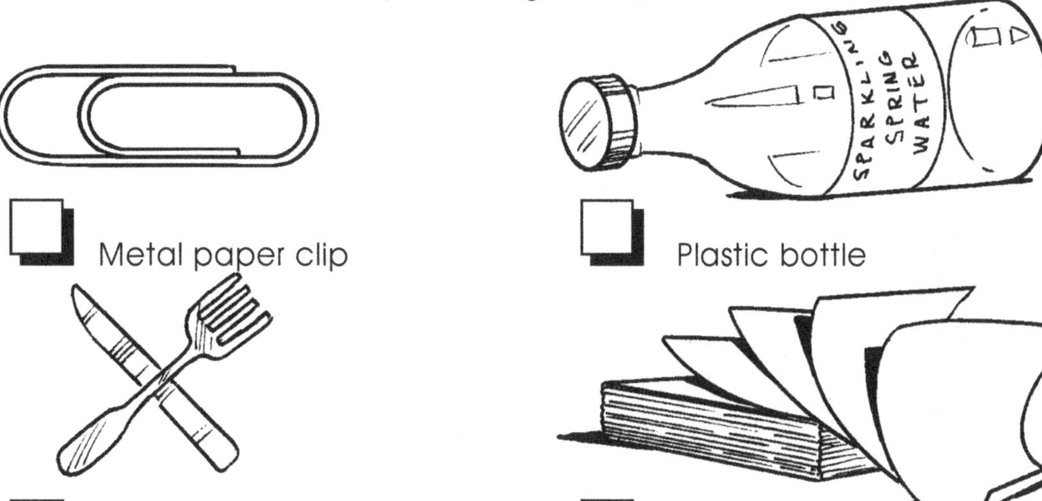

☐ Metal paper clip

☐ Plastic bottle

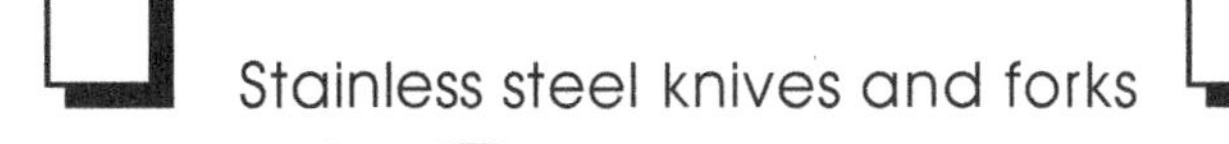

☐ Stainless steel knives and forks

☐ Paper

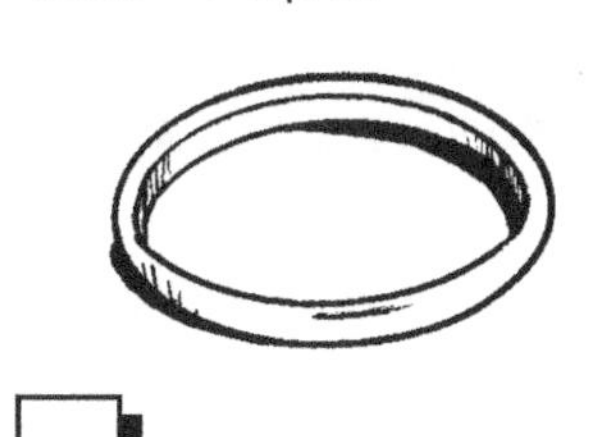

☐ Old car bodies

☐ Gold ring

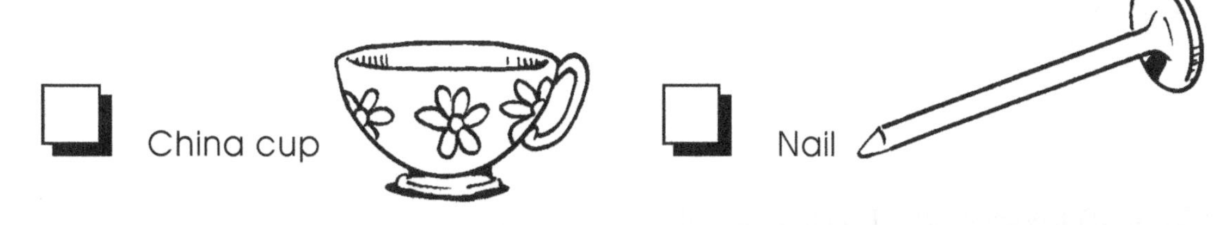

☐ China cup

☐ Nail

Think and do

What can be done to stop, or slow down, rusting?

Write or draw your answer.

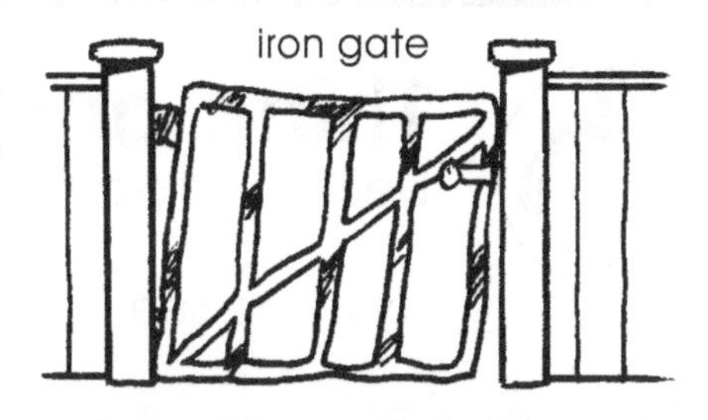

Dissolving

Read

Some things are **soluble**. This means they dissolve in water.
Other things are **insoluble**. They do not dissolve in water.

What to do

Put a tick ✓ in the box to show which things are **soluble** and which things are **insoluble**.

	Soluble	**Insoluble**
Sugar is	☐	☐
Coffee is	☐	☐
Hair is	☐	☐
Bread is	☐	☐
Margarine is	☐	☐
Orange juice is	☐	☐
Glass is	☐	☐
Skin is	☐	☐

You can investigate this if you wish.

Think and do

Does salt dissolve better in warm water or in cold water?

Try it and see.

Investigating dissolving

Investigate

Add one spoonful of white sugar to a glass of water.
Write or draw what happens.

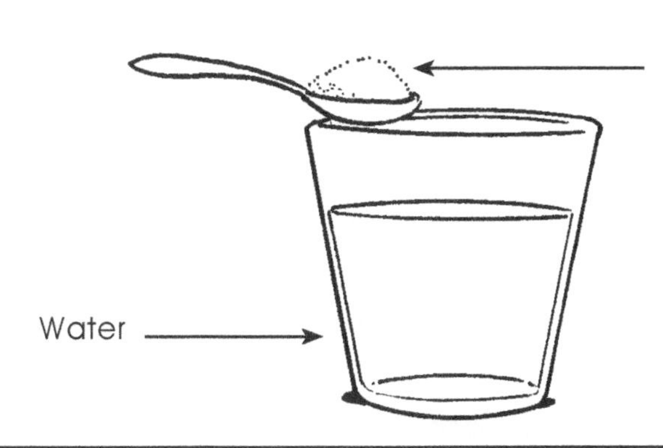

Is there a difference between how brown and white sugar dissolve in water? Yes/No

White sugar

Brown sugar

What is the difference?

....

....

....

Is there a difference if warm water is used? Yes/No

What is the difference?

....

....

....

Think and do

How does stirring help? Try it and see.

....

....

Drinking chocolate

Read

William had a drink of hot chocolate before going to sleep.
There was a little chocolate left in the cup. By morning it had 'dried up'.

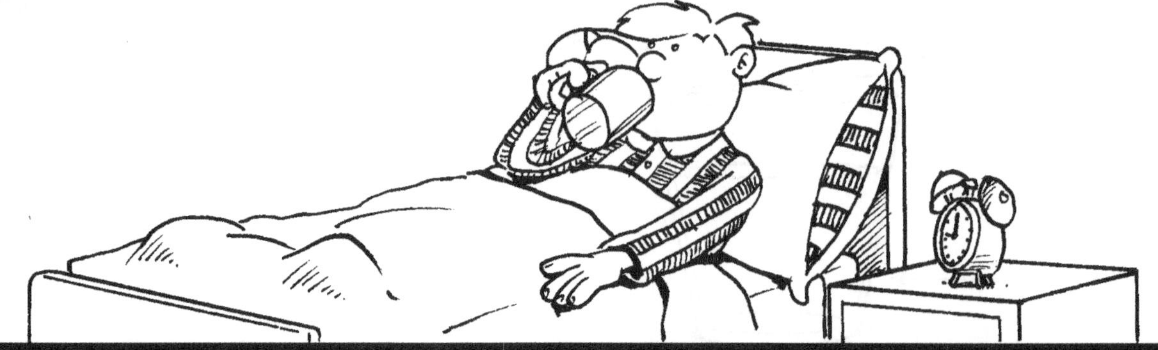

What to do

What has happened to the liquid?

. . . .

What has happened to the chocolate in the drink?

. . . .

William washes out the cup with warm water.

What happens to the chocolate?

. . . .

. . . .

Think and do

On the side of the tin of drinking chocolate it said it contained:

Food colour	Chocolate powder
Flavour	Sugar

What happens to all these things when the drink is made?

. . . .

What happens to the Smarties?

Investigate

Add one red Smartie to a glass of water. Do not stir.
Watch and draw what happens.

To another glass of water, add two different coloured Smarties.
Watch and draw what happens.

Was everything soluble? . . . .

Think and do

What do you think will happen when you try with other coloured Smarties?

. . . .

. . . .

. . . .

. . . .

Try it and see.

Tea bags

Read

A **filter** separates insoluble materials from liquids.

What to do

A tea bag has tea leaves inside a thin bag with small holes in it.
Draw how the colour and taste of the tea soaks through the bag.

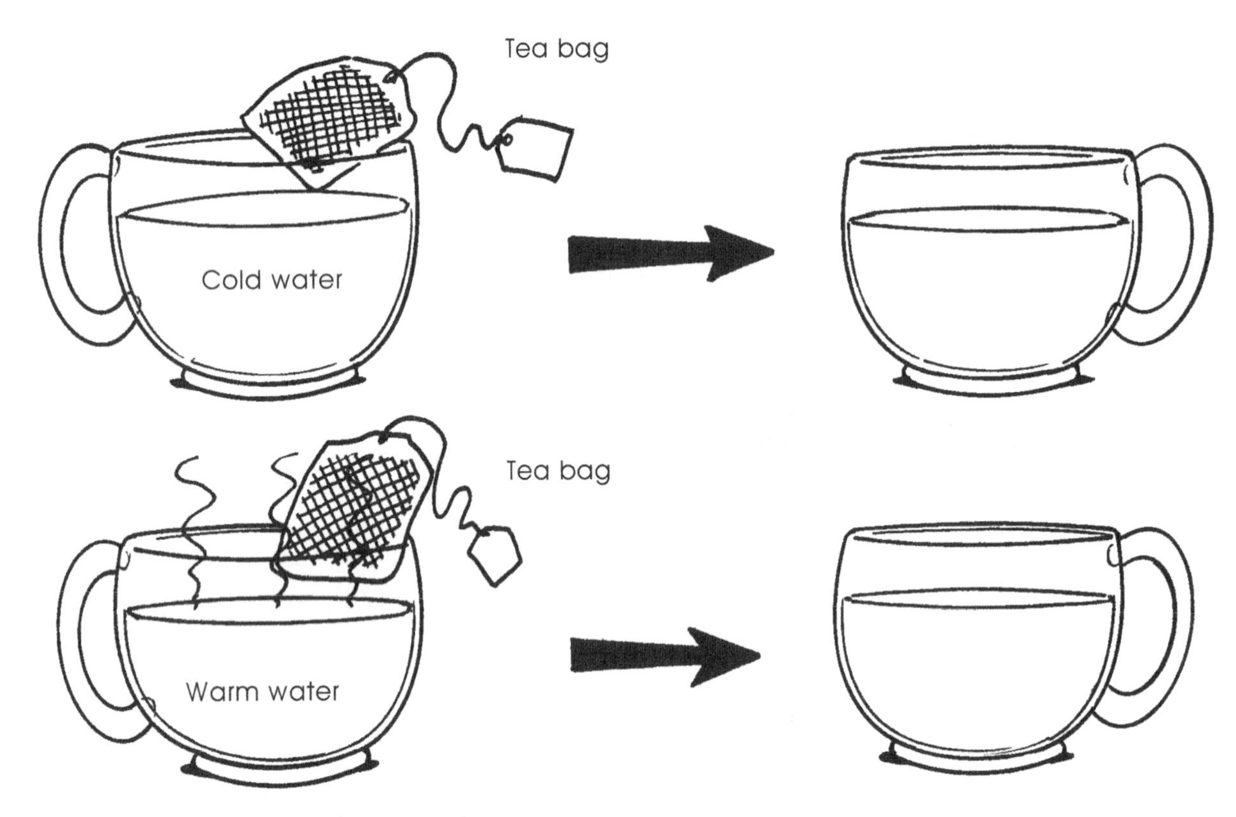

You can investigate this if you wish.

Think and do

What things in the tea bag are soluble in water? . . . .

. . . .

What things are insoluble?. . . . .

. . . .

What difference does it make using warm water? . . . .

. . . .

The material in the tea bag gives it the **t** _ _ _ _ and **c** _ _ _ _ _ .

Filtering

What to do

Razina makes coffee from powdered coffee beans and boiling water.

Choose the correct word to finish each sentence:

filters **residue** **dissolves**

The paper cone .... the soluble coffee from the beans.

The insoluble material left on the paper is called the ....

Part of the coffee bean .... and passes through the cone to give the flavour and taste.

Think and do

What is meant by **filtering**?

....

....

Can muddy water be filtered to make it clear? ....

Changes

Read

Some changes are easily **reversed** (changed back). Some are not.

What to do

Are these changes easily reversed?

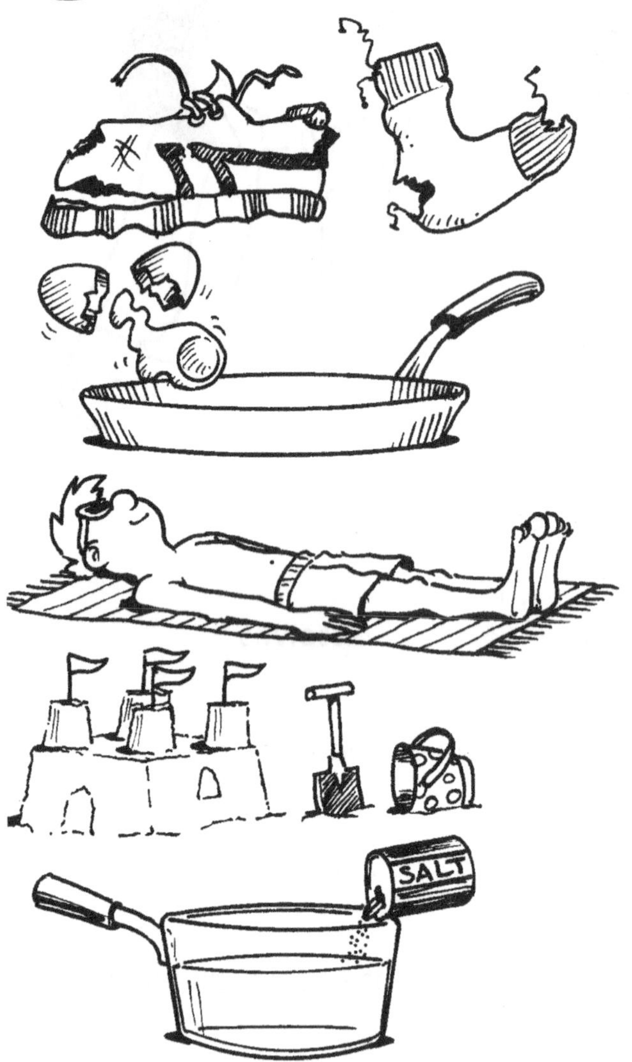

Write **Yes** or **No**.

Clothes that wear out

. . . .

Frying an egg

. . . .

Getting sunburnt

. . . .

Making a sandcastle

. . . .

Dissolving salt in water

. . . .

Think and do

Reversible changes can be changed back to where you started.
Non-reversible changes cannot be changed back.

Do you think eating food is reversible? Yes/No

Toasting bread

What to do

For breakfast Joe has a piece of toast.

Finish the drawing to show how toast is different from bread.

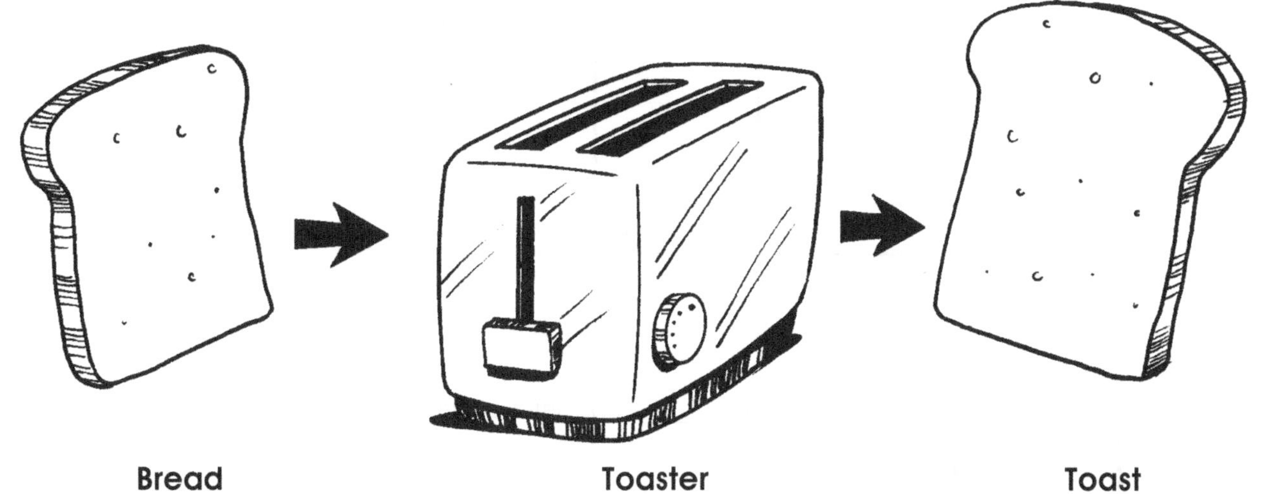

Bread **Toaster** **Toast**

Can you turn the toast back into bread? Yes/No

Draw what happens if a piece of fresh bread is left open to the air for a few weeks.

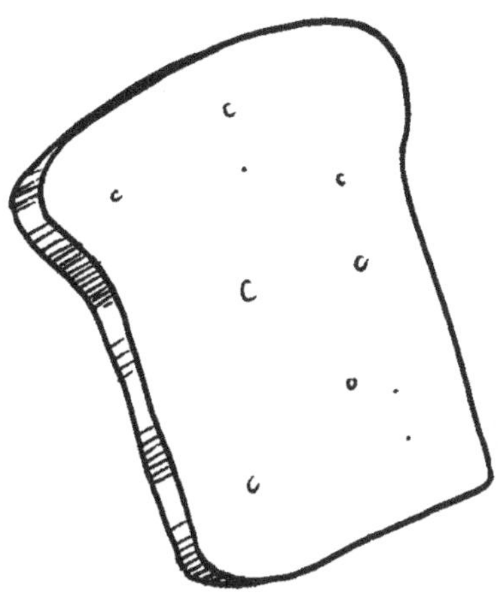

Bread before Bread after

Can you change these things back? Yes/No

Think and do

Are the changes that happen to the bread reversible or non-reversible?

. . . .

Changes to a flame

Investigate

Try this investigation.

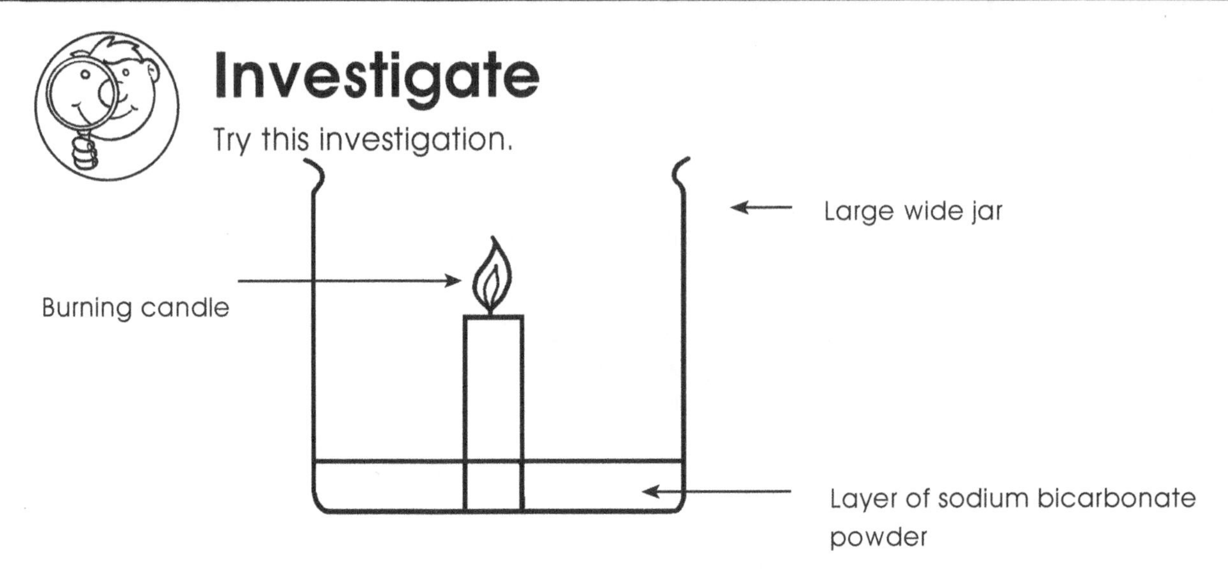

Add one spoonful of vinegar.

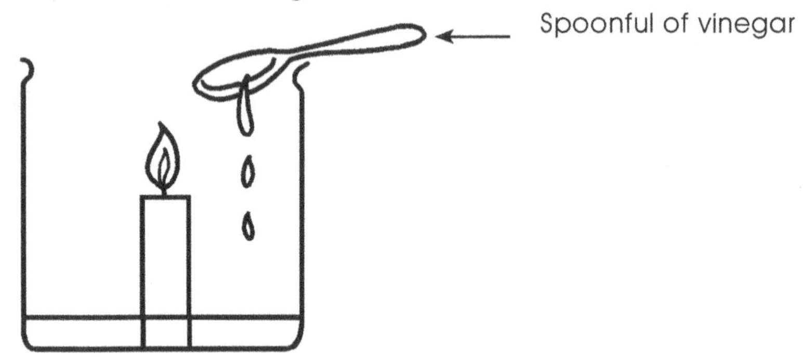

The sodium bicarbonate and vinegar fizz and give off carbon dioxide gas.

Draw what happens.

List things that changed:

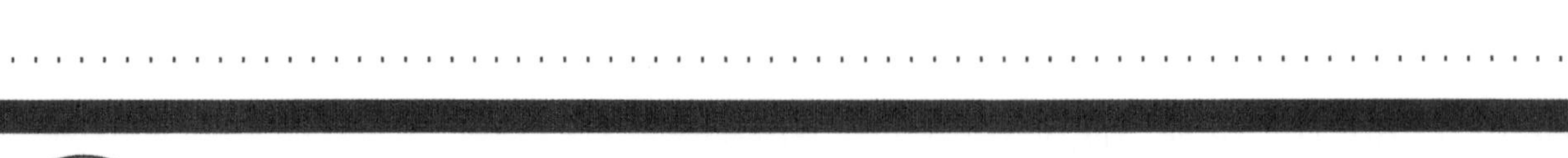

Think and do

What use could vinegar and sodium bicarbonate be put to?

. . . .

. . . .

What is changing?

What to do

Write what happens to the things in each picture.

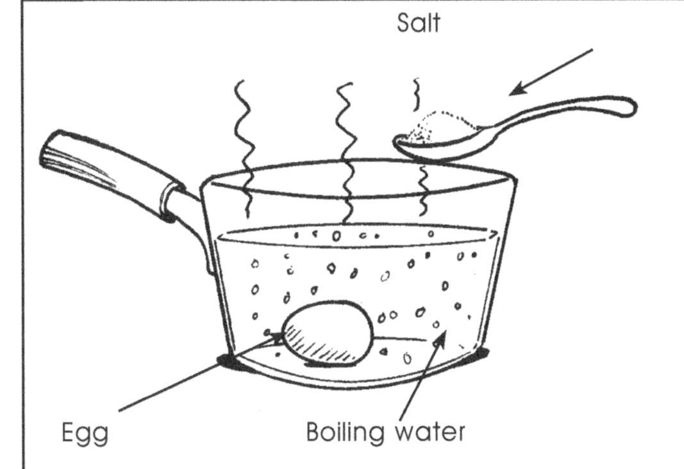

What happens to the ice?

. . . .

What happens to the water?

. . . .

What happens to the straw?

. . . .

Salt

Egg

Boiling water

What happens to the salt when added to the water?

. . . .

What happens to the boiling water if left?

. . . .

What happens to the egg?

. . . .

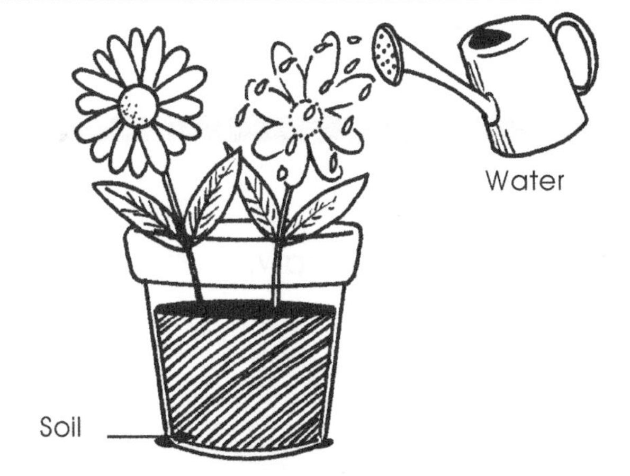

What happens to the water?

. . . .

. . . .

Think and do

Look at the pictures again.
Find two non-reversible changes that are happening.

1. . . . .

2. . . . .

Burning candles

What to do

Your teacher will light a candle. Watch it burning from a safe distance.

Draw lines from the words to the picture.

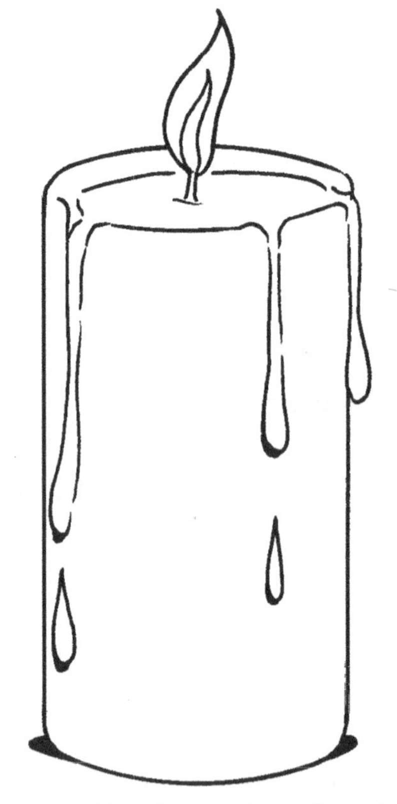

Pool of melted wax

Wick of candle

Yellow flame

Hot air above flame

Melted wax going solid down sides

Write or draw what happens when the flame is put out.

Think and do

Write out these sentences in the order of what you saw.

The wick was lit by the match.

The candle wax melted.

The match was lit.

The candle burned with a yellow flame.

What is in the bubbles?

Investigate

Half fill a bottle with water. Screw on the top. Shake for one minute. Draw what you see.

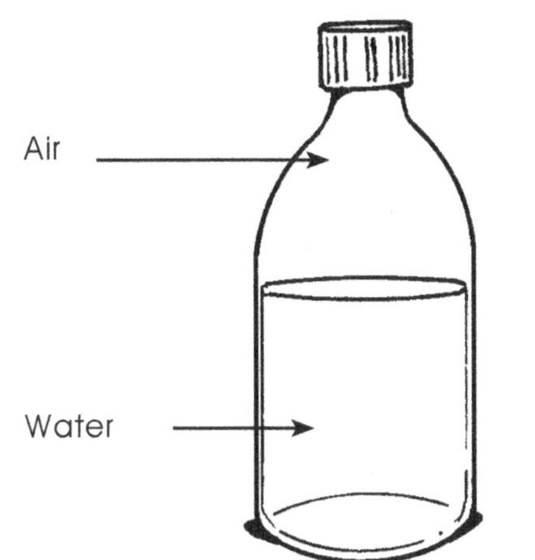

Shake bottle

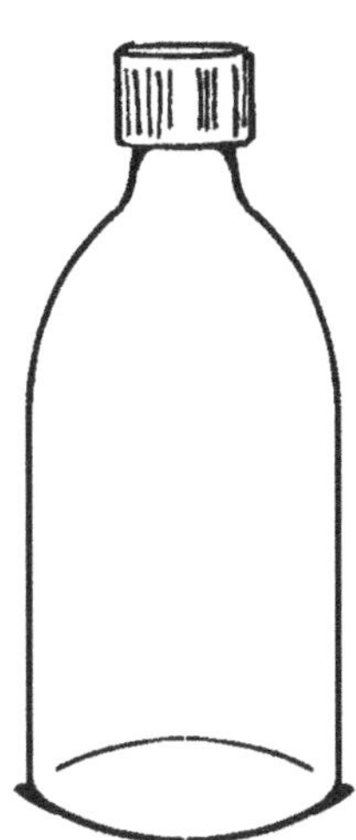

Are there any bubbles?

. . . .

Half fill a bottle with water. Add one drop of washing-up liquid. Screw on the top. Shake for one minute. Draw what you see.

How long do the bubbles last?

. . . .

What do you think is inside the bubbles?

. . . .

. . . .

Think and do

What could you add to the water to make the bubbles burst?

Salt

Sugar

Soap

A few drops of vinegar

Try the investigation before answering.

What is needed?

What to do

Put ticks ✓ to show what is needed by each of the following things.
(Some might need more than one tick.)

	Air	Water	Light	Food
Flower in pot				
Burning candle				
Cat				
Flying kite				
Fish				
Camera				
Tree				
Worm				

Think and do

Which of these things do **you** need?

☐ Air ☐ Water ☐ Light ☐ Food

Why? ....

Compost

Read

Compost-making is a slow, non-reversible change.
The materials change slowly into new, different ones.

What to do

Put a tick ✓ by the materials that you think will make good compost.

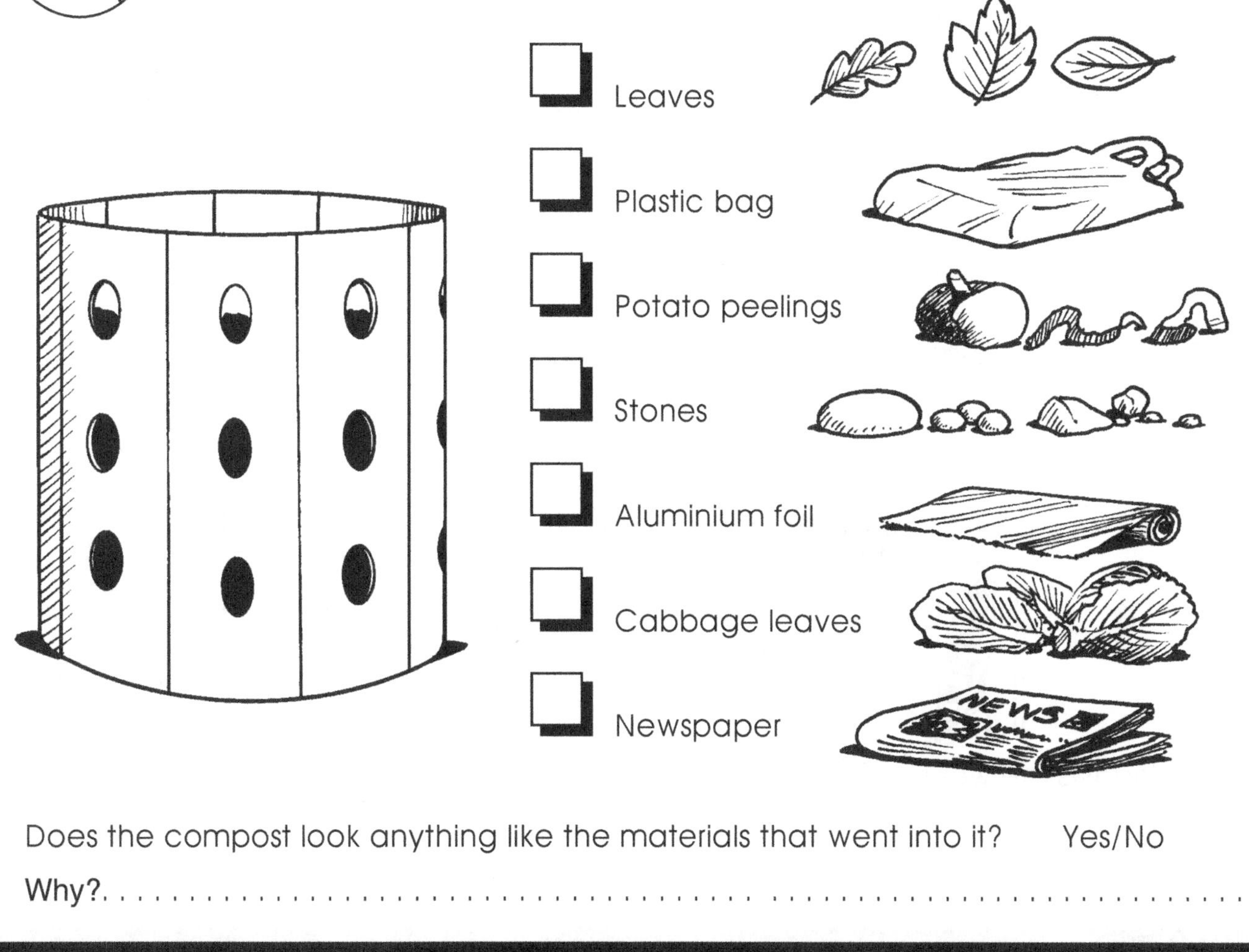

Does the compost look anything like the materials that went into it? Yes/No

Why?. . . . .

Think and do

What other things do you think are needed to make a good compost heap? (Hint: ask a gardener!)

. . . .

How do gardeners use compost in the garden?

. . . .

Water cycle

What to do

Kelly notices that, at bath-time, the cold windows get all 'steamed up'. Why?

The windows get 'steamed up' because:

What are the drops of liquid on the window?

In the winter Jack noticed that his bedroom windows are wet. Why?

The windows are wet because:

Think and do

Write or draw how you think rain-clouds are formed.

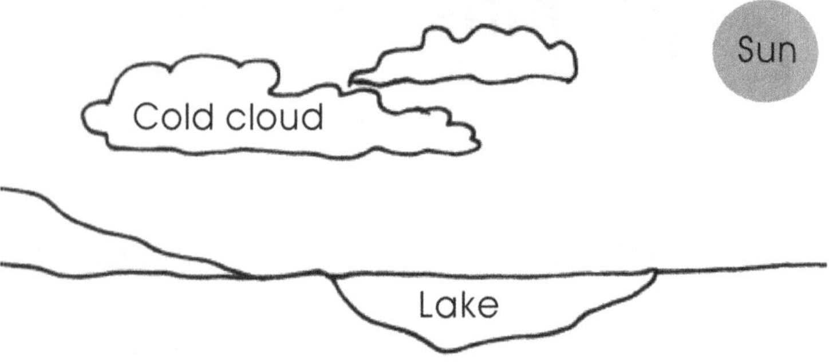

What happens?

What to do

Write what happens in each picture.

Lucy adds salt and potatoes to boiling water.

What happens to the potatoes?

. . . .

Which is soluble in water, salt or potatoes?

. . . .

Ravi waters a plant every day.

What happens to the water?

. . . .

Claire hangs wet washing on the line. It is windy.

What happens to the water?

. . . .

Sam uses a paper towel to mop up water.

What happens to the water?

. . . .

Think and do

Write or draw what you think happens to water when it goes down the plughole.

Snowman

Read

Jo and Di built a big snowman one winter.

What to do

The next morning the snowman had got smaller and it had icicles hanging from its nose and fingers. The scarf had gone all stiff.

What must have happened to the temperature overnight?

. . . .

. . . .

Where did the icicles come from?

. . . .

. . . .

Think and do

Draw what the snowman would look like if the sun came out.

Where does the snow go? . . . .

. . . .

Jelly and plaster

Read

Different materials have different properties.

What to do

Paul has a plaster cast on his arm. He is eating jelly.
Draw lines from some of the words to label the plaster cast and the jelly.

Hard

Soft

Made by mixing with water

See-through

Not see-through

Sets quickly

Sets hard

Sets wobbly

Think and do

Why do you think Paul's cast was made of plaster and not jelly?

. . . .

. . . .

The lost ring

Read

Sophie and Mark's mother has lost her wedding ring on the beach. Sophie and Mark help her to find it using their fishing net.

This beach has so much sand and so many stones. How am I going to find my ring?

What to do

Draw or write to show what you think they did.

1. First they ...	2. Then they ...
3. Then ...	4. At last! ...

Think and do

Can you think of two other ways to find the ring?

. . . .

. . . .

How much will dissolve?

Read

There is a limit to how much of a material will dissolve in water.
Different things dissolve in different amounts.

Investigate

Add one spoonful of sugar to a cup of warm water. Stir.
Will it dissolve? Yes/No

Keep adding sugar, one spoonful at a time, until no more dissolves.
Count how many spoonfuls you add.

I added .... spoonfuls of sugar until no more would dissolve in the water.

Now leave the sugar water open to the air for a few weeks. What happens?

....

....

Now try the same investigation with salt.
I added .... spoonfuls of salt until no more would dissolve in the water.

Which is the most soluble, salt or sugar?
Leave the salty water open to the air for a few weeks. What happens?

....

....

Think and do

Do you think the same amount of sugar and salt would dissolve in cold water?

....

Concrete

What to do

Andy was helping his dad to lay a concrete path.

These are the materials they used to make the concrete:

Sand

Water

Pebbles

Cement

Draw or write some instructions for them:

1. First ...	2. Then ...
3. Then ...	4. Lastly ...

Think and do

Give three ways that the concrete path is different from the materials it is made from.

1. ....

2. ....

3. ....

What other things can concrete be used for?

Hot and cold

What to do

Draw lines from the cups of liquids to the correct thermometers.
What are the readings on the thermometer?

Tap water

100°C

0°C

Iced water

100°C

0°C

Hot tea

100°C

0°C

Think and do

About what temperature would this thermometer read if it was placed under your arm?

60°C
50 ____________________
40
30
20
10
0

How hot has an oven got to be to cook a cake?

50°C   100°C   150°C   200°C

Gases in liquids

What to do

What are the gas bubbles in lemonade?

Put a tick ✓ or a cross ✖.

Air ❑

Carbon dioxide ❑

Oxygen ❑

When you buy a can of lemonade you buy the liquid, the can and the gas, which is dissolved in the lemonade.

What happens to the gas?. . . . .

At the end of the drink you have separated the solid . . . .

from the liquid . . . .

and the bubbles of . . . .

Where has the liquid and gas gone? . . . .

Think and do

Read and copy out what is written on the side of a can of cola about what is in it.

Problem solving, 1

What to do

Write or draw how you could help to solve these problems.

A sailor is stranded on a desert island. He wants to make drinking water from sea water. How can the sailor do it?

. . . .

. . . .

. . . .

. . . .

A farmer digs a well in his field. He wants fresh water, but the water has some small bits of dirt in it. How can he purify (clean) the water?

. . . .

. . . .

. . . .

. . . .

An engineer wants to find out if there are any iron girders in a wall of a house. She doesn't want to damage the wall. How can she find out?

Problem solving, 2

What to do

Look at the diagram. Work out a way to make the water level **A** fall. ↓
B rise. ↑

Write or draw your answers.

A. ....

....

B. ....

....

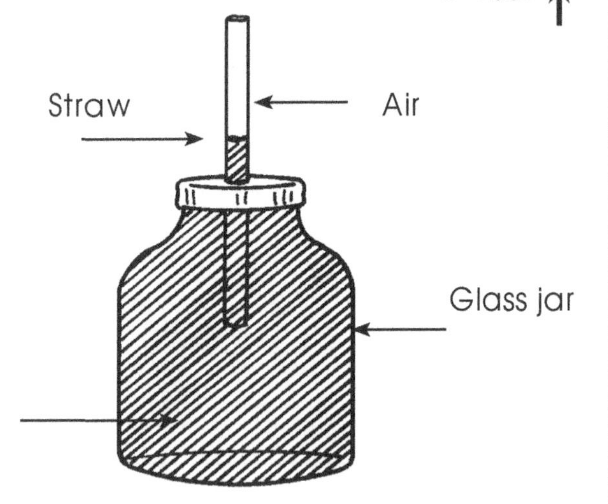

Look at the diagram. Write or draw what will happen to the wooden stick if the wire is heated with a candle.

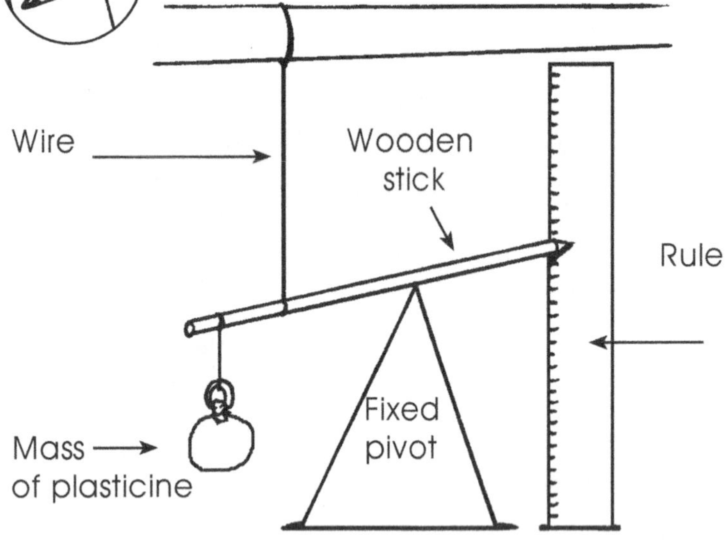

....

....

....

....

Think and do

What could the instruments in the pictures above be used to measure? How would you go about doing this?

....

....

Problem solving, 3

What to do

Look at the results of this experiment. Write and explain what has happened.

The candle has gone out because ...

. . . .

. . . .

. . . .

. . . .

Air

Water

What will happen to the water level as the ice cubes melt?

The water level will . . . .

because . . . .

. . . .

. . . .

. . . .

Try it and see if you were right.

What will happen to the balance as the ice cubes melt?

The balance will . . . .

. . . .

. . . .

. . . .

. . . .

Try it and see.

What to do

Look at the results of this investigation.

You will need tightly fitting, scew-topped jam jars and shiny nails.

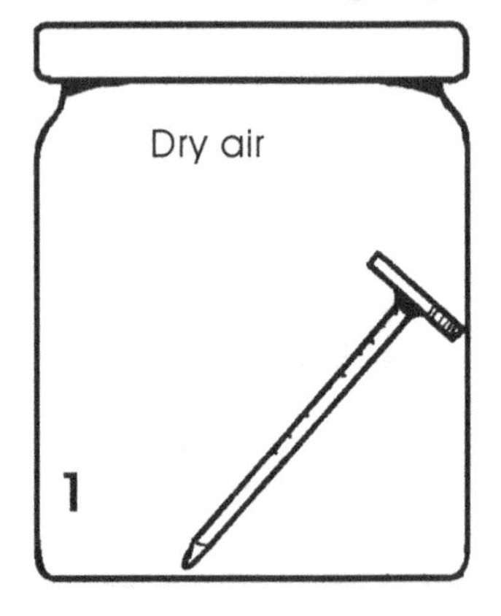

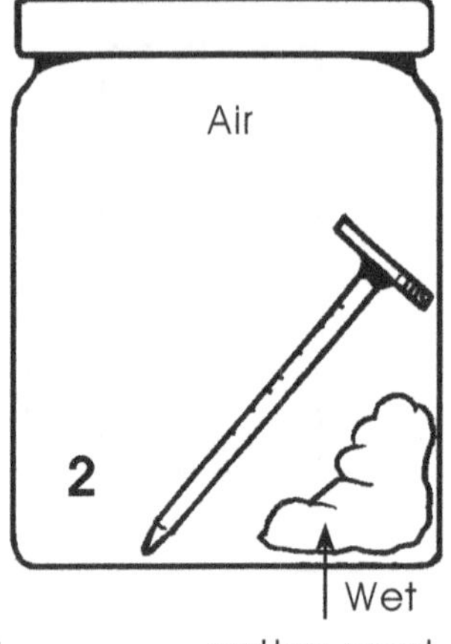

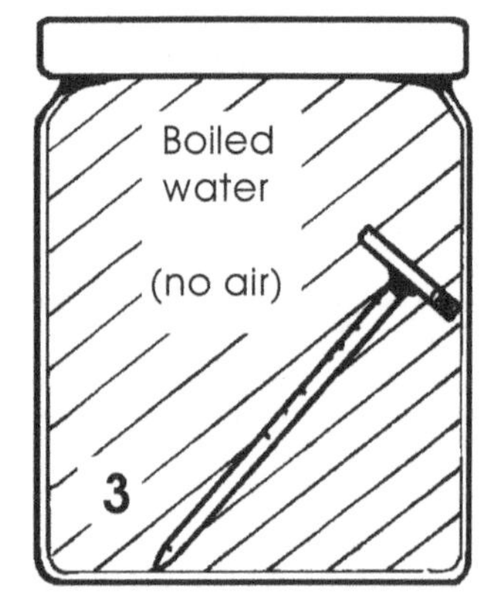

The nail in jar 2 went rusty.

Can you explain why?. . . . .

. . . .

On a cold winter's morning there are droplets of water on the inside of the bedroom window.

Where have they come from?

. . . .

. . . .

Look at this picture. What has caused the iron gate to go rusty? How can you stop it rusting?

. . . .

. . . .

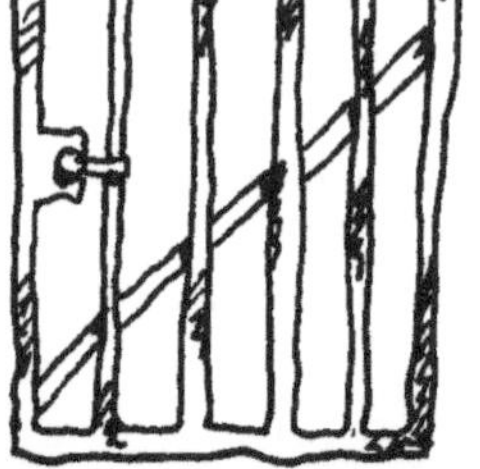

The limestone wall and the brick wall were built at the same time. Why has the limestone wall worn away more?

. . . .

. . . .

Rocks, 1

What to do

Look at the drawing of the mountain below. You can colour it in.

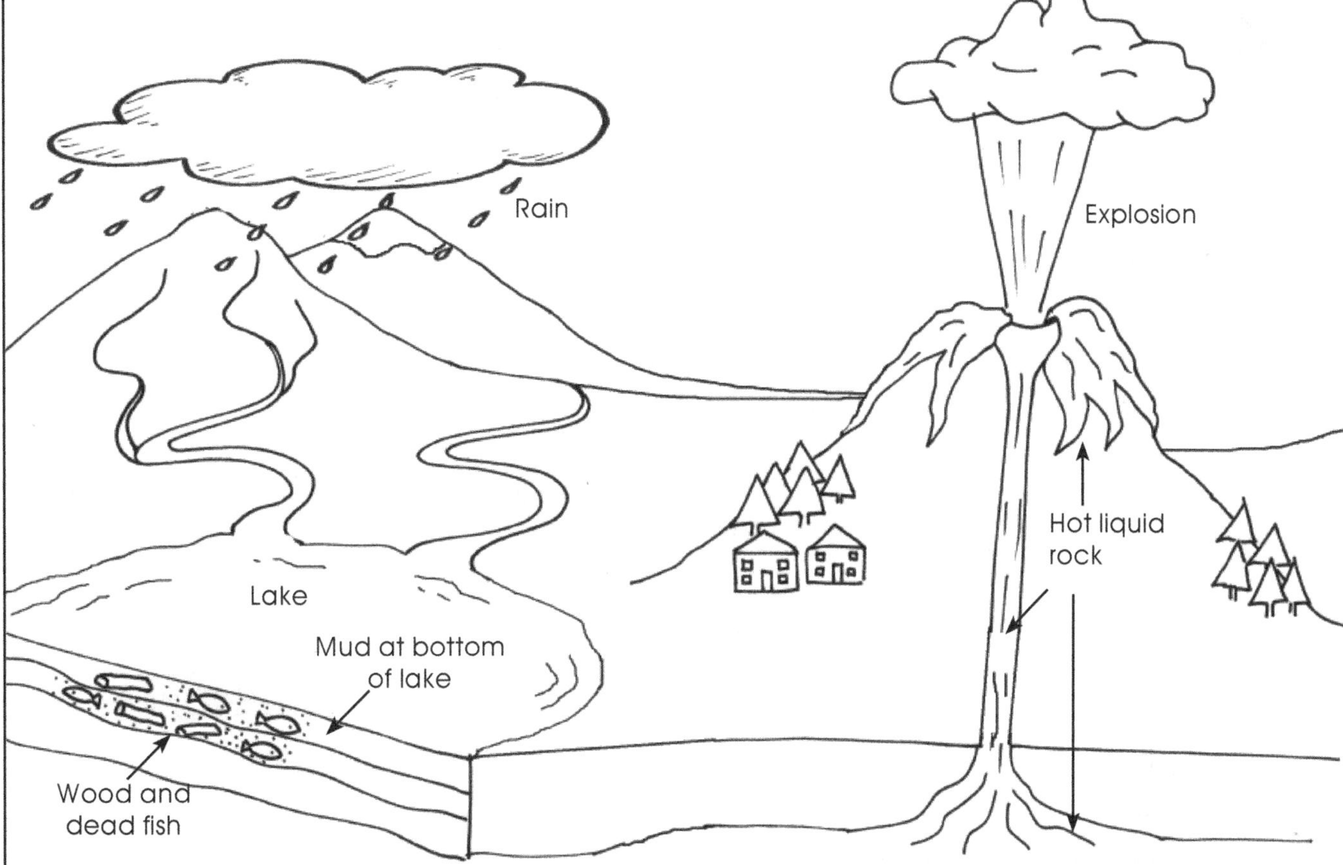

The exploding mountain is called a **V__ L __ A __O .**

The hot liquid rock inside the mountain is called **M __ G __ A .**

The liquid rock flowing down the side of the mountain is called **L __ V __ .**

Think and do

What happens to the rock and dust blown out of the top of the mountain?

Where did the hot liquid rock come from?

What would happen to the trees and houses when the hot flowing lava reaches it?

After a long time, the buried logs, fish and shells at the bottom of the lake will turn into **F __ __ __ __ __ __ .**

Use the Internet to find photos of a volcano.

Rocks, 2

Read

Joe's hobby is rock collecting. Look at some of the stones he has collected.

1. Smooth pebble

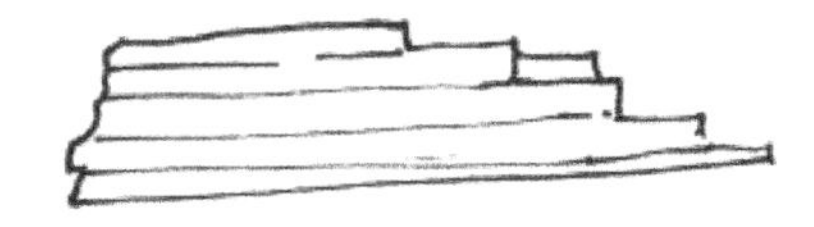

2. Thin slate

3. Crystals

4. Coal

5. Snail shape squashed into the stone

6. Different coloured sand

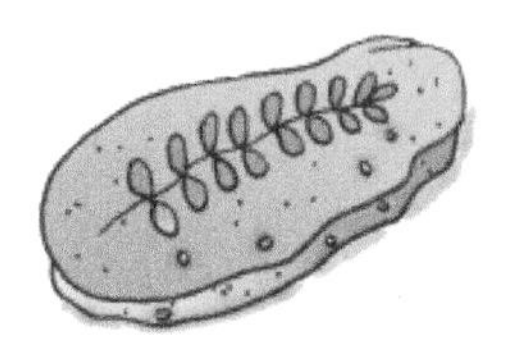

7. Leaf squashed into a stone

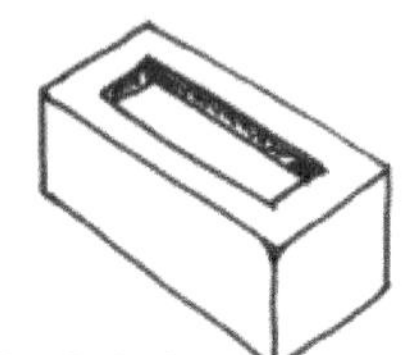

8. Brick

9. Road stone

Which rocks can be found on the sea shore? ....

Which ones are fossils? ....

How were fossils formed? ....

Which rocks are used for building houses? ....

Think and do

How did the leaf and snail shape get into the rock?

....

How was the coal formed? ....

When the magma cools very slowly underground, sometimes crystals can be formed. Which stone in Joe's collection could have formed that way? ....

Rocks, 3

Think and do

When rain and snow fall on the mountain rocks they break up into smaller pieces.

What then happens to these pieces?

Why is the soil in some areas of the country a different colour?

Some mountain rocks are very hard and can be polished. What could these be used for?

When a stream or river flows over some stones or rocks for a long time, what happens to them?

Some old walls, stone statues and grave stones wear away. What causes this?

Joe found a piece of coal with a leaf print in it. What does that say about how coal was formed?

Road stones are made of (hard/soft) stones so that they do not ______________ when cars run over them.

Rocks 3 continued

What will happen if a piece of blackboard chalk is left out in the rain for a long time?

. . . .

. . . .

What does all this tell you about the rocks?

. . . .

. . . .

Draw and explain how the water vapour turns back into clouds to form rain. You might include words like:

evaporation	Sun's heat	condensation
cold	cloud	water cycle

. . . .

. . . .

. . . .

. . . .

Lightning Source UK Ltd.
Milton Keynes UK
UKOW06f0122230914

238973UK00004B/49/P

9 781783 170968